INSIDE SPECIAL FORCES ™

SPECIAL OPS:
TACTICAL TRAINING

Mary Blount Christian

rosen publishing's
rosen
central

New York

Published in 2015 by The Rosen Publishing Group, Inc.
29 East 21st Street, New York, NY 10010

Library of Congress Cataloging-in-Publication Data

Christian, Mary Blount.
Special ops: tactical training/Mary Blount Christian.—First edition.
    pages cm.—(Inside Special Forces)
Includes bibliographical references and index.
ISBN 978-1-4777-7547-9 (library bound)—ISBN 978-1-4777-7549-3 (pbk.) —
ISBN 978-1-4777-7550-9 (6-pack)
1. Special forces (Military science)—Juvenile literature. 2. Special operations
(Military science)—United States—History—Juvenile literature. I. Title.
UA34.S64C49 2014
356'.16—dc23
                                                                    2014012123

Manufactured in Malaysia

CONTENTS

INTRODUCTION

You are jammed shoulder-to-shoulder, face-to-face, with another chalk of grim-faced men. The helmet and night-vision goggles weigh heavily on your head. You want to shift your legs, but you can't. The ruck is already firmly strapped between them.

It's cold, but sweat beads form above your lips. Nerves, probably. Failure is not an option. The vibration of the plane is like an electrical pulse through your body, but the noise of the engine reassures you—when the noise stops, it's time to worry.

First, you had to get Basic Training and Jump School out of the way. As it turned out, they weren't the piece of cake you had anticipated. From the 5:00 AM bugle wake-up call to the 9:30 PM "Taps," you had to process enormous amounts of information and endure arduous physical activities. Those morning runs before school and physical training (PT) under your football coach's watchful eye were nothing.

To get to your final exam, you've waded through swamps, survived sand fleas, carried your weight in gear, and forgot that you were once an individual. You've become stronger and more determined than you thought possible. And you've done it all so you can call yourself a Special Operator.

The plane's engines sound different. The speed slows. The jumpmaster removes the door. Air rushes in. The green light comes on. You stand and inch

Special Ops Forces require candidates to receive jump training so that they can exit aircraft like this C-130J Super Hercules.

forward, your toes to the other guy's heels, waddling like a duck with the rucksack between your legs.

You see the men step through the door and disappear. You take a deep breath and step into the abyss. It's black as pitch, and you forget to flip down your night-vision goggles.

You have just stepped from the aircraft 10,000 feet (3,048 meters) above Earth with 100 pounds (45.4 kilograms) of survival gear strapped between your legs.

You slash through the air like a hot knife through butter at 100 miles (161 kilometers) per hour. The only sounds you hear are the beats of your heart and the wind rushing past you.

Every survival instinct tells you to pull the ripcord, but your training says wait, wait—now! The parachute opens with a snap, and your body jerks into an upright position. The canopy swells with air, and your speed slows. That's one what-if out of the way. But how many more to go?

If your goal is to join any of the Special Operations Forces (Special Ops) of the United States military, you will have to endure many such grueling steps as part of your training. Special Ops units engage in nontraditional forms of warfare and must be prepared to use specialized skills in a wide range of missions. Selection and training varies across the Special Ops Forces but always goes well beyond the weeks of Boot Camp and Jump School. For the most part, only men are allowed to join. Every one of the Special Ops Forces—including the Green Berets, Rangers, Navy SEALs, Airborne (Night Stalkers), Air Force Special Operations, Marine Corps Forces Special Operations, and Delta, which chooses a few of the best from any branch and makes them even tougher—requires a rigorous training process that often only a select few can complete. But those who succeed can count themselves among an elite group with a prominent role to play in the wake of changing warfare.

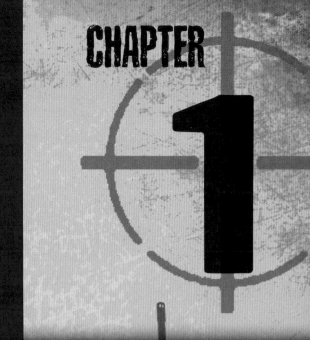

CHAPTER 1

STEPPING ON AIR

You're hanging from your parachute floating toward Earth. It's a pleasant sensation, probably the last you'll experience for some time. You can't relax, though. Where will you land: a body of water, a stand of trees, or in the heart of an enemy camp? Anything is possible. A thousand what-if scenarios clutter your thinking.

You are not alone. Eleven others in your ODA (Operational Detachment Alpha) are in slow descent beside you. These guys have been with you from day one in this Special Ops unit.

Below is Pineland, where hostages are waiting. So are the enemy and their sympathizers. How will you know the difference? Besides your buddies, whom can you trust? Make a wrong judgment, and you are done. Months of mental and physical training, which some consider torture, will be for nothing.

BOOTS ON THE GROUND

Your feet touch ground. You whip off the helmet that protected you during the high-altitude drop. You release the rucksack strapped to your legs. Quiet as a whisper, you crush the air from your parachute and hide it in the underbrush. The opposition force must not know you are here.

Your senses are on high alert. Silence is as revealing as sound. It means movement nearby —but is it friendly or hostile? With your map and compass, you cautiously head to the rendezvous one click (one mile, or 1,609 m) away.

That small voice in your head says, "Leave no tracks. Turn no blade of grass, break no twig, and bend no branch." Leave nothing for enemy patrols to spot.

NO PLACE FOR RAMBO

All present and accounted for. These men trained with you. They are the only ones you fully trust. The leader relates the mission known as Operation Robin Sage. Quash the enemy, destroy their communications, and free the people of Pineland.

You will spend the next two weeks using every covert skill you learned during the months of training so harsh it made grown men cry. Only in movies do soldiers rush in blindly with weapons firing. You will use psychology, diplomacy, and negotiation to identify local freedom fighters, or guerrillas. Once inside enemy territory, you will identify disaffected groups, those people who are not happy with the current social conditions.

You will muster them into a guerrilla fighting force. They will provide intelligence and safe houses. If the village needs water, you will dig a well. If the villagers need food, you will provide it. Make friends. But make no mistake. Enemies hide among them. They will lie to you. They will turn you over to the opposition.

You remind yourself to watch for the telltale signs. Watch their eyes and their demeanor. You will know if they are lying. Ferret out the opposition force and its sympathizers. Don't get caught.

BUT IT SEEMS SO REAL

No one is in real danger—this time. The ammunition is not real. Nor is the foreign country. You have landed in Uwharrie National Forest, 4,500 acres that stretch across Montgomery, Randolph, and Davidson Counties in North Carolina.

For more than fifty years, five generations

A veil of red smoke obscures the approach of soldiers during Operation Robin Sage in Uwharrie National Forest.

of North Carolinians have pretended to be patriots or enemy sympathizers in a foreign country. Veterans and current members of the Army Special Forces play guerrillas or opposition forces. Instructors observe the applicants as they spend two weeks achieving their mission. This is the final exam for the remaining 20 percent of applicants to the U.S. Army Special Forces, the elite Green Berets.

The training sent eighty out of one hundred applicants back to the regular army ranks. The final exam will cull out another 10 percent. Outside of a real mission, this is the hardest physical and mental challenge an applicant will face.

Even after enduring the months of training, some will be dropped at the end of Operation Robin Sage. Everything they learned must come together at one time. There is no room in Special Operations for having a bad day. But there is no disgrace in washing out of any of the military branches' Special Ops Forces. Men will return to their units better trained and in better physical condition than any other in their ranks. They may remain and become leaders or try again in a year. Although applicants to other Special Ops Forces will experience different final tests, much of the same will hold true for them.

Special Ops personnel are never idle. When they are not on a mission, they are training for one. The public may never hear of most of their missions, at least not until the government is ready to provide details. Even then, the details may be sketchy,

Belly-crawling through the mud under barbed wire is only one part of the "Nasty Nick" Army Special Forces obstacle course. It takes exceptional physical condition to make it in any Special Ops branch.

and the identities of some Special Operators may remain secret.

Operation Robin Sage is the last time those Operators will know for sure that the danger is not real. For those who graduate, life will never be quite the same. A day off from work will never be relaxing. From this day forward, their pagers will be their constant accessories. No matter where they are or what they are doing, when it rings, they will drop everything, grab their gear, and report to the base.

Special Operators won't be able to tell anyone about their missions. That date you have finally landed won't know why you don't show up or why you can't say that you're possibly thousands of miles away.

It won't be until you are airborne over the ocean that you hear those words that make your adrenaline rise: "This is not a drill."

EVERY BRANCH HAS ITS OWN SPECIAL OPS FORCES

At first glance, it may seem that all of the Special Ops Forces are alike—they are small units that strike quickly, neutralize a situation, and withdraw before the opposition has time to react. The differences may seem subtle, but they are vital to successful missions. The legend goes that you can put a representative of each branch in a room together with the task of deciding which is best. But don't wait for a consensus any time soon. No one is going to surrender.

The Army has several Special Ops Forces, the most famous of which are: the U.S. Army Special Forces (Green Berets); Army Rangers; the 160th Special Operations Aviation Regiment (SOAR), better known as Night Stalkers; and the 1st Special Forces Operational Detachment-Delta, or Delta Force. Other well-known military Special Ops groups include the Navy SEALs, the Marine Special Command (MARSOC), and the Air Force Special Operations Command. All of the above are under the United States Special Operations

Missions take Special Ops Forces all over the world. Soldiers from the 1st Special Forces Group (Airborne) and the Republic of Korea 11th Special Forces Brigade cover each other during annual training exercises near Gwangyang, South Korea.

Command (SOCOM), headquartered at MacDill Air Force Base in Tampa, Florida.

Delta Force selects the best of the best. If you still have your heart set on becoming a member of the Delta Force, you will need to take everything you have learned in any other Special Ops Force and double it. Many of those who try out for Delta Force are already Army Rangers or Green Berets, though other members of the U.S. military may volunteer as

SERE: A FORMULA FOR SURVIVAL ANYWHERE IN THE WORLD

All Special Ops Forces in every branch of the military live by a code of behavior that they maintain regardless of the difficult circumstances they may face. Survival, Evasion, Resistance, and Escape, or "SERE," is an intense military training program that Special Ops personnel and others, such as aviators, must complete to learn—as the name suggests—survival and escape skills.

Special Operators risk capture inside enemy lines. They learn camouflage, woodcraft, and how to make tools to survive in hostile environments amid the enemy. Whether it is in frigid territory with little but ice and snow or in arid deserts with no water in sight, they learn to improvise and innovate their way through every challenge. Trainees make fire by friction, fire by mirrors, and even fire by ice (by using the heat of their hands to mold the ice into a lens, which works just like a magnifying glass) if they are operating in arctic-like areas.

In mock POW camps, trainees are hooded, blindfolded, mistreated, and pushed to the breaking point to learn to resist torture. They train to escape and aid others to escape captivity. But instruction can't predict everything that may come up when they are on their own. Special Operators learn how to think on their feet and leave no man behind.

well. The details of the grueling mental and physical training remain unknown to the public. Delta Force candidates must pass the calisthenics, the 3-mile (4.8 km) run, the all-night, 18-mile (29 km) hike over mountain terrain with a 35-pound (15.9 kg) backpack and a compass, and the 40-mile (64.4 km) hike with a 45-pound (20.4 kg) backpack in even less time. Psychologists test applicants with a battery of mental exams designed to break them. Pass that, and they can begin Delta Force training with no guarantees. That's a little of what it takes to be in Delta, or as members refer to it, "The Unit." It is the only Special Ops Force officially dedicated to hostage rescues, counter-insurgency, and general counterterrorism.

2

LIKE PEAS IN A POD?

The protest you'll hear is, "We are not hats; we are soldiers, men!" Yet, thanks to movies, their song, tales of heroism, and their signature headgear, members of the U.S. Army Special Forces are forever known to the public as Green Berets.

A member of the U.S. Army Special Forces wears the Green Beret, which was authorized in 1961 by President John F. Kennedy.

CIVILIANS WELCOME (FOR MEN ONLY)

Recruits to Special Forces are no longer restricted to already enlisted personnel. Although it is subject to change, depending on the army's need for specialty expertise, for the first time in many years, male civilians may apply to the Army Special Forces. Official websites or local recruiters are the best source for the most up-to-date requirements.

Even if civilians have an in-demand specialty, they also need to be in excellent physical condition. They will compete for a few positions with already seasoned soldiers and eligible non-commissioned ("non-com") and commissioned officers.

The Army Special Forces and the Army Rangers are not the same, although they both begin with the same basic Boot Camp training and train at the same Jump School. But their deployments differ, as does their training. After candidates complete Basic Combat Training, they attend Infantry School as part of their Advanced Individual Training (AIT), where they learn about various weapons, from small arms to howitzers and heavy mortars.

WHEN THEY SAY JUMP...

Airborne School at Fort Benning, which follows AIT, consists of three weeks of training and is a requirement for members of any service. During training, students learn how to jump from a plane using a parachute, which is the fastest way to exit an aircraft. Anyone who doesn't mind that first giant step

SOLDIER OR CIVILIAN, THE REQUIREMENTS ARE THE SAME

All applicants to the Army Special Forces must pass the Special Forces Assessment and Selection Course (SFAS) and meet certain requirements to be accepted into the course. They must be males between twenty and thirty years old, U.S. citizens, and at least high school graduates (a GED doesn't count). Because their job demands that they adapt to different areas of the world, Green Berets are often college educated, some to a post-graduate level. Many applicants are already bilingual. Their near and distant vision in both eyes must be naturally or corrected to 20/20, and they must pass the required Army Physical Fitness Assessment (PFA).

Applicants must qualify for a secret security clearance and achieve a General Technical score of 107 or higher and a combat operation score of 98 or higher on the Armed Services Vocational Aptitude Battery. Applicants must be airborne-ready (graduated from the three-week Jump School) or be working on it at Airborne School at Fort Benning, Georgia.

can jump, but it's the safe landing that requires some practice. Trainees are eased into it, starting with ground-level practice that uses simulated plane doors on platforms and progressing to jumping with full gear and a rifle from a real plane.

During Ground Week, trainees learn how to perfect a Parachute Landing Fall (PLF), where they are trained how to land and properly distribute energy throughout their legs in order to prevent injury.

Trainees first jump at ground level to practice their landing technique. They begin by jumping into sand or pebble pits from platforms of different heights while they are suspended on wires. Instructors (called the Black Hats, for obvious reasons) watch every move and tell the trainees what they are doing wrong.

At the end of the week, trainees jump from a 34-foot (10.4 m) tower—the equivalent of a two-story building—using a lateral drift apparatus (LDA), a device that consists of a descending cable that students grasp and then release, practicing a PLF on the way down.

Some of the applicants will have to repeat the week ("recycle," they call it), because only the physically fit and successful will move forward.

YOU MEAN THERE'S MORE?

After passing Ground Week, trainees must go through Tower Week, where they learn the different phases of parachute flight. Before the week is over, candidates are required to jump from towers of different heights and prepare for various scenarios that

These Jump School students have already passed Ground Week. During the second week, Tower Week, they practice safely exiting through a mock door at the top of a 34-foot (10.4 m) tower.

may occur during an actual jump. Additionally, they must pass all PT requirements with ruck runs, push-ups, sit-ups, and pull-ups. By the end of the week, they will know how to exit an aircraft with a team in an orderly way.

Jump Week follows Tower Week. During that time, a trainee must complete five jumps from an aircraft at 1,250 feet (381 m). One of these jumps is a night jump. Only after completing all jumps will a trainee graduate Airborne School. During Jump Week, trainees will jump without a load, with a full combat load, and in other configurations.

After successfully completing five qualifying jumps by the end of Jump Week, trainees receive the "Silver Wing" on their uniform.

SFAS AND BEYOND

Even after graduating Airborne School, there is no time to sit back and reflect or nurse those sore muscles. So far, you have only achieved what is required of every member of the military. If you aspire to be a Green Beret, you are off to the Special Operations Preparation Course, a thirty-day course at Fort Bragg, North Carolina, which provides physical training and land-navigation training for the Special Forces Assessment and Selection Course (SFAS). The SFAS is a three-week course, where trainees are exposed to grueling physical tests, including long marches in extreme weather conditions with heavy packs; obstacle courses that test their ability to climb walls or navigate underground pipes; problem-solving with minimal sleep, often at night and during a long march; and PT, which includes running, swimming, push-ups, pull-ups, and sit-ups. A trainee must prove that he is both a leader and a team player. Those who pass the SFAS will go on to the Special Forces Qualification Course (SFQC, or Q Course), which can last anywhere from six

During the three-week SFAS Course, candidates must demonstrate teamwork and physical endurance in various situations, like carrying this heavy makeshift litter over obstacles.

months to more than a year, depending on the trainee's specialty. Those who do not pass SFAS may take the course again or rejoin the army branch in which they started.

The Q Course includes five phases, each dedicated to one of the following areas: Small Unit Tactics, Military Occupational Specialty (MOS) Training, Collective Training, Language and Culture, and Graduation. The SERE survival skills of candidates will be tested through various exercises during the first phase, and they will also learn counterinsurgency, advanced marksmanship, how to react in live fire, and other skills.

Candidates begin to hone the skills specific to the specialty they've chosen during the second phase. Specialty fields include officer training, weapons training, medical training, engineering, communications, and operations/intelligence. The third phase is largely spent preparing for and enduring the fifteen-day Operation Robin Sage in which candidate must manage an onslaught of challenges through Pineland. This test is the most difficult portion of the Q Course. Even candidates who pass this stage are not quite finished with training yet, though—they must also be trained in the culture, language, customs, geography, and traditions of the area that will ultimately serve as their Area of Operation (AO) during the fourth phase. Green Berets are assigned to one of five areas around the world. Only after this twenty-four-week course will the candidates officially be Green Berets and sport the headgear for which they worked so hard.

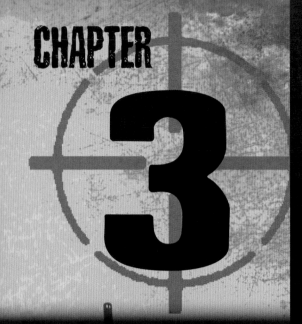

U.S. ARMY RANGERS

A soldier rappels down a wall at the U.S. Army Ranger School at Ft. Benning, Georgia, where candidates face many grueling challenges.

You have completed the nine weeks of Basic Combat Training, Airborne, and Advanced Individual Training. It's time to forget about days off. Forget about sleep, and forget about that rewarding slice of apple pie à la mode you've dreamed about. You are in for the challenges of endurance, intelligence, mental agility, and stamina like never before.

If you want to be an Army Ranger, you will head to the Army Ranger School at Fort Benning, Georgia, and face tough months ahead. The bus is waiting, so grab your gear and that bottle of liniment. All aboard!

PATROLS ARE NO STROLL IN THE PARK

You may be in the school, but you aren't a Ranger yet. With your previous physical training, you traded fat for muscle, and you feel leaner and stronger than any other time in your life. But from now on, wherever you go, you will walk double-time in your boots with everything you own strapped to your back. Your gear goes with you—everywhere.

Even when you are on patrol with others and must share the load of a log, you must still bear your own rucksack, rifle, and ammo. While patrolling more than 200 miles (322 km) during the course, you will add an additional 40 pounds (18.1 kg) of weapons, equipment, and ammo. At any moment, you may additionally have to man one corner of a stretcher for a comrade who is playing dead or wounded. And if you are the one playing dead that day and feel like you are the lucky one who is carried, remember that the guys holding that stretcher are every bit as tired as you are. You could wind up seriously wounded if one drops from exhaustion.

YOU HAVE TO CRAWL BEFORE YOU WALK

The first of three phases in Ranger School is called the Fort Benning, or "Crawl" Phase. Candidates begin this phase with the standard Ranger Physical Assessment test, which consists of a minimum of forty-nine push-ups, fifty-nine sit-ups, six pull-ups, and a 5-mile (8 km) run in forty minutes or less. At a minimum, candidates need to perform at this level in order to achieve a score of seventy points for each event. Many candidates recycle (repeat) at least one phase, so they can have more than one shot at it.

Phase 1 lasts twenty days and is divided into two parts. The first part, which lasts the first four days of Ranger School, is called the Ranger Assessment Phase (RAP) and is commonly called RAP Week. RAP Week will challenge your mental and physical abilities. The Ranger Physical Assessment test is only one part of it. You must also pass the Combat Water Survival Assessment, more 5-mile (8 km) runs, an event called the Darby Mile Run, the Malvesti obstacle course, run over rough terrain, complete a 12-mile (19.3 km) foot march, and accomplish land navigation in day and night, and that's after being awake for twenty-four hours. If you're caught slipping in a little nap, you may have washed out, but you won't know it until the end of the course. At the least, you are "dead" for the remainder of the test and earn no points.

All the while, the officers and psychologists are evaluating your mental and physical endurance as surprises and challenges are thrown at you. You'll also take demolition and airborne refresher training.

It sounds rough—and it is—but this training is designed to prepare applicants for the psychological stress and physical fatigue experienced in combat. Over half of the candidates who wash out of Ranger School do so in the first four days because they fail one of these events.

SLEEPLESS AND HUNGRY IS A WAY OF LIFE

The second part of this first phase includes the Darby Queen Obstacle Course and long ruck marches. You will also learn the fundamentals of patrolling and small-unit tactics. You'll be graded on how you handle ambush and reconnaissance patrols, close-quarters combat, and airborne operations. You will need to demonstrate expertise in cadre and student-led tactical patrol operations. The leadership role may fall on you at any moment.

Throughout the Crawl Phase, you will experience twenty-hour days with only one or two meals and an average of three and a half hours of sleep. When you have to jump, you will get a little extra sleep time for safety's sake. You will run 5 miles (8 km) three or four times a week and swim in your uniform two or three times a week. Expect to lose weight, as you will eat only once or twice a day, despite your physical exertion, and have maybe fifteen minutes to eat all you can. You will work twenty out of twenty-four hours every day. By the end of Phase 1, you should be able to successfully complete somewhere between 80 and 100 push-ups, 80 to 100 sit-ups, 15 to 20 chin-ups, and run 2 miles (3.2 km) in thirteen minutes.

RUN, BUT BE PREPARED TO SWIM

If you haven't given up or washed out with injuries by now, you will head for the Florida, or "Run,"

WALKING IS ONLY THE HALF OF IT

Rangers live by their motto: "A Ranger Never Quits." This motto will be tested dearly during the second phase of training.

During the first phase, you will only cover rugged, fairly flat terrain. The second phase, the Mountain or "Walk" Phase, takes place in the mountains at Camp Merrill in Georgia and lasts for a period of twenty-one days. Soldiers must survive dangerous conditions and hostile terrain. They must also demonstrate that they can handle physically and emotionally challenging situations while sleep deprived and hungry.

Students will learn military mountaineering, which includes climbing, rappelling, and tying knots. They must also engage in various patrol, combat, and raid scenarios. You'll be expected to endure all of these extreme situations for three weeks

Ranger candidates pick their way through rocks and up a mountain during the twenty-one-day Mountain Phase at Camp Merrill, Georgia.

while sustaining yourself on only one or two MREs (Meals, Ready to Eat). Statistics show that 94 percent of those who begin Phase 2 eventually move to the third phase.

Phase, which is the third and final phase of Ranger School. This phase continues to develop the Ranger students' combat and arms skills with no let-up of the extreme mental and physical stress of the first two phases. You will perform extended platoon-level patrol operations in a swamp environment in Florida. You will train to lead small units on airborne, air assault, small boat, ship-to-shore, and dismounted combat-patrol operations. You must demonstrate quick thinking and ingenuity because you are up against a formidable enemy.

During the Run Phase, you will spend long hours walking with your full gear, sleeping in the field, and living on one or two MREs (Meals, Ready to Eat) a day for eighteen days. All the while, you will face surprise ambushes, simulated attacks, and other combat scenarios. Survive that, and you can wear the Ranger patch and tan beret. But don't think that you will be resting and regaining your weight in that time. Once you gain the necessary skills, you will hone them daily.

If you are a warrant officer or senior non-com (Staff Sergeant through Sergeant Major), you will endure another three weeks of the Ranger Assessment and Selection Program so that you will be able to spot

Trainees conduct a small boat maneuver at Camp Rudder, Florida, during the Run Phase. Rangers may have to use these skills during an actual covert mission.

the best leadership talent in the army ranks. There are hundreds of qualified Rangers, and one full battalion is on high alert at all times, ready to be boots-on-the-ground anywhere in the world within eighteen hours. Special Ops may perform thousands of quick raids, but they operate in the shadows, and the public will never know. They like it that way.

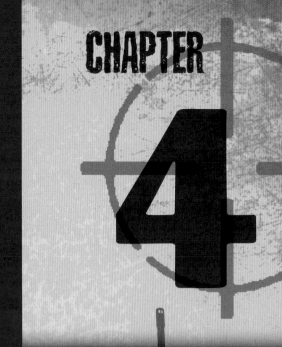

TWO IF BY SEA

While the Coast Guard operates in the waters surrounding the United States, the Navy SEALs take care of interests else-where in the world. They get their name not because they are as at home in the water as the sea mammal, but because they are trained to operate at sea, in the air, and on land.

SEAL candidates must be male U.S. citizens of good moral character between eighteen and twenty-eight years old with a high school edu-cation or GED. They may come from navy or Coast Guard ranks. Their vision should be at least 20/75 and correctible to 20/20.

The SEAL Prep Course takes place in Chi-cago, Illinois, and lasts eight weeks. It begins and ends with Physical Screening Tests. If you pass the entry level Physical Screening Test, you will move to a more demanding test that includes a timed 4-mile (6.4 km) run and a timed 1,000-meter (3,281 foot) swim. The goal is to push an applicant to his physical and mental limits in preparation for the extreme physical and mental challenges of SEAL missions. If you succeed, you are ready to move on to Basic Underwater Demolition School (BUD/S).

THE ONLY EASY DAY WAS YESTERDAY

BUD/S is a twenty-four-week course to push your mental and physical boundaries, develop teamwork and leadership skills, test your pain thresholds, and gauge your determination. SEAL recruits begin in Coronado, California, where they complete three weeks of orientation to get used to their new lifestyle and the regimen that their instructors expect from them. Trainees learn that the motto, "The Only Easy Day Was Yesterday," is not without meaning.

Phase 1, Physical Conditioning, lasts another seven weeks. It includes running, swimming, and calisthenics that get increasingly more difficult. The first three weeks will seem simple when you hit Hell Week, the fourth week, which includes five and a half days of non-stop training with a total of only four hours sleep.

At any given time, you will be expected to perform some type of physical activity. You may spend long periods of time in the cold ocean, trudge through mud and sand, paddle boats, carry heavy logs or boats overhead, or perform PT-like sit-ups or push-ups, all while coping with extreme exhaustion, sleep deprivation, and possibly hypothermia. Only around 25 percent of recruits pass Hell Week—and those who do are still not done.

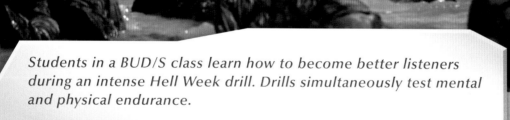

Students in a BUD/S class learn how to become better listeners during an intense Hell Week drill. Drills simultaneously test mental and physical endurance.

During the remainder of Phase 1, you will learn hydrographic surveys and charts, and you will be assessed on water competency, teamwork, and mental tenacity.

EVERYONE INTO THE WATER

Phase 2 is the Diving Phase, which lasts seven weeks. By the end of this phase, recruits should become competent basic-combat swimmers. Physical training

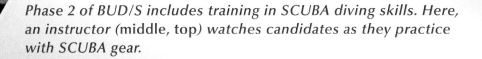

Phase 2 of BUD/S includes training in SCUBA diving skills. Here, an instructor (middle, top) watches candidates as they practice with SCUBA gear.

becomes even tougher. Recruits will receive intensive training on SCUBA (Self Contained Underwater Breathing Apparatus) equipment and diving, as well as on underwater combat, which is what separates SEALs from all of the other Special Operations Forces.

BECAUSE SOME TARGETS ARE LAND-LOCKED

Land Warfare training comprises Phase 3 and lasts another seven weeks. By the end of this phase, you will be qualified in basic weapons, demolition, and small-unit tactics. Your physical training will become even more strenuous as you will be required to run farther in less time. You will also be required to swim certain distances and complete an obstacle course in less time than before.

This third phase trains you in land navigation, working in small units, patrolling, and rappelling. You'll also work on your marksmanship and both how to find and work with military explosives. You spend the last three and a half weeks on San Clemente Island in California, where you will demonstrate what you have learned.

As part of BUD/S land navigation training, candidates learn to read maps, plot courses, and navigate. SEAL operations are not limited to the water.

UP, UP, AND AWAY!

Once you have successfully completed BUD/S, you will attend the accelerated three-week Parachute Jump School in San Diego, California. SEAL candidates will work up to jumping from a minimum altitude of 9,500 feet (2,896 m) with combat equipment. They will have to learn how to jump from various heights in varying conditions and also how to jump at night. A strict regimen is designed to ensure that SEAL candidates can become safe free-fall jumpers in just three weeks.

OPPORTUNITIES FOR MORE ADVANCEMENT

Advanced training possibilities include foreign language study, SEAL tactical communications training, sniper, military free-fall parachuting, jump master (static line and military free fall), explosive breacher, and much more. Those who have a medical rating will attend Advanced Medical Training Course 18D for six months at Fort Bragg, North Carolina, to become a SEAL medic.

If you are a SEAL with a college degree, you may attend the Junior Officer Training Course to learn operations planning and how to lead team briefings.

FIT, BUT NOT FIT FOR DUTY—YET!

Even after all you have been through, you are still not finished. You've proven yourself exceptional in physical and mental ability, but you have more to prove in order to add "warrior" to your resume. You have another twenty-six weeks in Coronado for SEAL Qualification Training (SQT). Advanced Sea, Air, and Land Training includes cold-water survival, marine operations, advanced combat swimming, close-quarter combat, and land warfare in mountains, woodlands, and jungle, arctic, or desert conditions. You will learn how to operate both as an individual and as part of a platoon. The Navy SEAL Trident is awarded to graduates of SQT, who then begin advanced training and receive their assignment to a SEAL team.

You'll report to your First SEAL Team or Special Delivery Vehicle (SDV) Team at Virginia Beach, Virginia; Pearl Harbor, Hawaii; or Coronado, California, for eighteen months of advanced training divided equally between Individual Specialty Training, Unit Level Training, and Task Group Level Training. SEAL Teams 1–5 and 7–10 are designated by different colors. Their missions remain within specific regions. SEAL Team 6 (the team that completed the raid of Osama bin Laden's compound in Pakistan) is also called Rainbow; it is the only one that goes anywhere in the world.

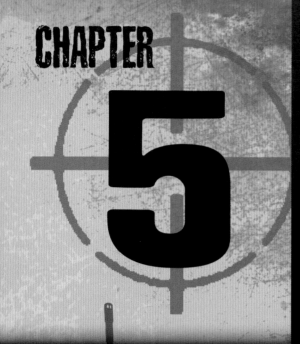

MARINE SPECIAL OPERATIONS COMMAND

The U.S. Marine Corps has its own Special Operations Force. Marine Special Operations Command (MARSOC) missions are similar to other special operations in that they take place in irregular and unconventional settings. MARSOC applicants receive additional training with Special Operations Equipment and Tactics.

For those Marine candidates who enlist east of the Mississippi River, Boot Camp is at the Recruit Training Depot at Parris Island, South Carolina. Those who enlist west of the Mississippi attend Boot Camp in San Diego, California. Recruits receive full medical and dental screenings and take the Initial Strength Test.

To pass (and avoid the Physical Conditioning Platoon), recruits must successfully complete two dead-hang pull-ups and forty-four sit-ups

At the Marine Corps Recruit Depot in San Diego, California, recruits begin an 880-yard (804.6 m) run as part of the Combat Fitness Test, a test all Marines must complete each year.

in two minutes, and a 1.5-mile (2.4 km) run in thirteen and a half minutes. Before you graduate, you'll also have to demonstrate basic swimming skills.

REMEMBER WHEN YOU USED TO SLEEP?

You'll spend the entire first night of Boot Camp and all of the next day awake just so you can complete paperwork processing, have your hair cut off, and turn in all of the civilian clothing and articles you own (including eyeglasses and contact lenses, which will be replaced by regulation glasses).

NEW ENGLISH DICTIONARY, MARINE VERSION

From day one, you must learn how to speak Marine—no slip-ups. Instead of going upstairs, you go "topside." Downstairs is now "down below." Your bunk becomes a "rack." The latrine is a "head." The floor is a "deck." The walls are "bulkheads." The buildings no longer have windows or a ceiling, but "portholes" and "overhead." You can still face "forward," but behind you is "aft." To your left is "port," and on your right is "starboard." Your Drill Instructor's office must be called the "Drill Instructor House."

Words to wipe from your vocabulary are the pronouns. From now on, speak in third person only. Refer to yourself as "this recruit" instead of "me" or "I." It's "these recruits" or "those recruits" instead of "us" or "we." Most important, don't use the word "you" when speaking to the Drill Instructor. It is either "Sir" or "the Drill Instructor."

From here on out, everything happens when and how your instructors tell you, including the simple process of going to the head (bathroom) and showering: 1. Line up; 2. March to showerhead; 3. Pull the ring and wet your head; 4. Soap your head and face thoroughly; 5. Rinse, etc.

To volunteer to become a MARSOC Operator, you must have a minimum General Technical (GT) score of 105 and a minimum Physical Fitness Test score of 225 and pass the MARSOC swim assessment, which you can view in an online film. You must meet all of the criteria of the medical screen and be eligible for a secret security clearance. If you are selected (and to be sure, you will need to excel beyond the minimums listed), you must be willing to make a lateral move to critical-skills operator.

THE CRUCIBLE IS A CRUCIAL STEP

The Crucible is a rite of passage that tests every Marine recruit physically, mentally, and morally and takes place over fifty-four hours. Recruits must march more than 45 miles (72.4 km) on little food and sleep. Teams of recruits face a variety of day and night events where they must work together to solve problems, overcome obstacles including long marches,

The object of this Crucible exercise is to move the barrel over the wall without touching any of the red squares. Failure means a 100-yard (91.4 m) run with 30-pound (13.6 kg) ammunition cans.

41

and complete combat assault courses, a leadership reaction course, and team-building warrior stations emphasizing the values Marines champion. Those who pass the Crucible are qualified to be Marines, but to be a part of MARSOC, recruits must endure additional screening, testing, and training.

VIS GREGIS EST LUPUS

MARSOC deploys forces worldwide to perform missions assigned by U.S. Special Operations Command (USSOCOM). Candidates will first undergo a selection process, and those who continue will attend the Marine Special Operations Individual Training Course (ITC) at the Marine Special Operations School (MSOS) at Camp Lejeune, North Carolina. The ITC is a seven-month course that screens, trains, and assesses applicants' skills.

You will go through Assessment and Selection first—nineteen days of mentally and physically demanding tasks with no guarantee that you'll continue. Aside from the physical training, which includes increasingly difficult running, swimming, and hiking, you will also receive instruction in basic Marine Corps and MARSOC principles that you will apply in practice. A ten-week training guide and access to the MARSOC website will help you prepare for the physical-fitness aspects of the assessment and selection process. There is also a three-week preparation course for the Assessment phase.

Those who move on—as either Critical Skills Operators (CSOs) or Special Operations Officers—will be assigned to an ITC class, where they will be expected to live up to the ITC motto: *Vis Gregis Est Lupus* ("The strength of the pack is the wolf"). They will begin with Phase 1, a ten-week course that builds on basic individual fitness skills, such as swimming, running, rucking (running with full gear pack), fire support, tactical casualty care, and hand-to-hand combat with training in such disciplines as Jeet Kune Do, Wing Chun, Karate, Jiu-Jitsu, and even Pankration and Sayoc Kali (Filipino knife fighting). Applicants will improve on patrolling, mission planning, fire support, land navigation, and combat medic training. They will also have SERE training during this phase.

Phase 2 is comprised of eight weeks of training in small-unit tactics. Candidates will train in intelligence gathering and learn how to navigate on water, handle small boats, and operate in both rural and urban settings. Exercises

MARSOC sponsors a Jane Wayne Day at Camp Lejeune, North Carolina, at which wives experience how Critical Skills Operators prepare for missions with patrols, an obstacle course, rides on zodiac boats, and a simulated raid.

will test them on reconnaissance, patrol, and combat operations.

During Phase 3, students will focus on what is called precision training. They will learn Close Quarters Combat (CQC) and marksmanship using rifles and pistons. This training hones in on the skills MARSOC Operators would use during actual assault operations. Students will learn how to work with a team to shoot and move through a target and will also master communications using various types of systems, ranging from high-frequency radio to satellite. This phase lasts five weeks.

Phase 4, the final phase of training, is dedicated to training students in asymmetric, or irregular, warfare—warfare in which the military power of one side far exceeds the military power of the other. This phase lasts seven weeks. The final exercise, called "Operation Derna Bridge," requires students to apply all of the skills they acquired during training. They must advise a partner nation and learn how to train and operate with an irregular force.

Those who graduate will be assigned to one of the three Marine Special Operations Battalions (MSOB). After receiving their assignments, CSOs who qualify can receive additional training. Advanced training in combat, parachuting, diving, languages, sniper shooting, helicopter rope suspension, and SERE are just some of the options offered.

IT'S NOT OVER UNTIL IT'S OVER

ITC is designed to create versatile Operators who are willing and capable of any special operation they are called upon to do under Special Operations Command. Marines must learn how to think like the enemy. If they can anticipate their enemies' actions, they can stop them before they happen.

Special Operations training takes what Marines learned during Basic Training and magnifies it, increasing the physical and mental pressure until recruits are tougher than the average leatherneck, and that says a lot. *Semper Fi.*

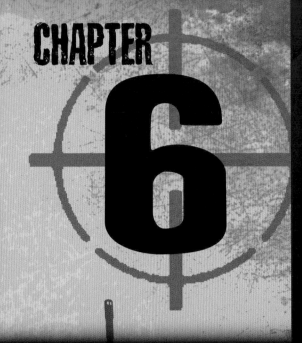

CHAPTER 6

WHEN LIVES DEPEND ON THEM

None of the Special Operations Forces could do their jobs if they were unable get to scenes of conflict that are oceans, or at least many miles, away. Two Special Operations Forces take care of that.

The first is the army's 160th SOAR(A), or 160th Special Operations Aviation Regiment (Airborne), better known as Night Stalkers. Named for their proficiency at night, they accept male and female aviators who have accumulated at least five hundred flight hours in flight school. On short notice, they provide stealth curb service at targets, day or night, using modified Chinook, Black Hawk, and Little Bird helicopters.

The second is the U.S. Air Force Special Tactics with its three teams: Combat Control (CCT), Pararescue (PJ), and Special Operations Weathermen.

Members of the army's 160th SOAR(A) are trained to fly aircraft, such as this Black Hawk helicopter, in all types of weather to any location in the world. They often operate at night.

COMBAT CONTROLLERS

Combat Controllers are Federal Aviation Administration (FAA)–certified air traffic controllers—the same as those civilian ATCs at your local airport. The difference is that Combat Controllers are additionally combat ready.

NOT YOUR CONTROL TOWER KIND OF GUYS

Combat Controllers are among the most highly trained specialists in the U.S. military. They must maintain FAA air traffic control qualification throughout their military careers. Should they retire from the military, they are certified to step into the high-volume control towers at any airport in the United States.

To safely control aircraft near or behind enemy lines, Combat Controllers must first get there and establish communications. They are trained to be combat ready, like any other soldier. They may have to fight their way in, set up their equipment, and guide the aviators in at the same time. If they successfully pass thirty-five weeks of training for their missions, they wear a scarlet beret.

Combat Controllers attend a one-week orientation at Lackland Air Force Base in San Antonio, Texas. There, they learn about sports physiology, nutrition, basic exercises, and the history and fundamentals of Combat Control Tactics.

From there, they head to Keesler Air Force Base (AFB) in Biloxi, Mississippi, where they attend a fifteen and a half–week Combat Control Operator Course, which includes training in aircraft recognition, air navigation aids, weather, and other topics. Training also includes airport traffic control and rules, flight assistance, communication procedures, conventional approach control, and radar procedures.

This training is identical to the course for civilian air traffic controllers.

From Keesler, trainees attend the one course no one gets to skip: Jump School at U.S. Army Airborne School at Fort Benning, Georgia, where they learn how to perform an airdrop into a target area. After completing the same mandatory three weeks (Ground, Tower, and Jump), trainees head to the U.S. Air Force Basic Survival School at Fairchild AFB in Spokane, Washington. There, they will spend two and a half weeks learning the equipment and skills to survive in severe weather conditions and hostile environments.

Combat Control School at Fort Bragg's Pope Field northwest of Fayetteville, North Carolina, is the last stop before graduation. There, students spend eighty-four days qualifying in physical training, small unit tactics, land navigation, communications, assault zones, demolitions, fire support, and field operations. If you pass, you can wear that scarlet beret—but you aren't through yet.

CAN YOU SPARE A YEAR?

Expect more travel when you go into the Special Tactics Advanced Skills Training (AST) that begins at Hurlburt Field in Pensacola, Florida. This twelve-month course requires students to complete demanding mental and physical training in four phases: water, ground, control experience, and full-mission understanding.

Before you're finished, you'll attend U.S. Army Military Free Fall Parachutist School at Fort Bragg, North

Carolina, and Yuma Proving Grounds, Arizona, for five weeks to perfect free-fall parachuting procedures. You will have four weeks at U.S. Army Special Forces Combat Divers School in Key West, Florida, to learn SCUBA and covert infiltration under various operating conditions at depths of 130 feet (39.6 m).

At the U.S. Navy Underwater Egress Training at Pensacola Naval Air Station, Florida, you will learn to safely escape from an aircraft that has landed in the water.

THESE EMTS GO ANYWHERE FOR PATIENTS

Parachute Jumpers (PJs) are combat-ready rescue and recovery specialists certified as emergency medical technicians (EMTs). They receive the same training as those who operate civilian ambulances, but PJs must either rappel or parachute to their patients.

PJs have requirements similar to their civilian counterparts, but need specialized and intensive training in order to be combat ready. They train in parachuting, combat scuba diving, rapelling, skiing, motorcycling, and the survival skills necessary to handle any environment and situation. If you opt for Pararescue, you will complete the same technical training as EMT Paramedics, plus additional physical and specialized training at the nine-week Indoctrination Course at Lackland AFB. PJs undergo extensive physical conditioning and physiological training and must endure an obstacle course, rucksack marches, and courses in dive physics, dive tables, and various medical procedures. They also receive training in

PJs prepare extensively so that they can reach the wounded under any circumstance. In addition to parachute training, candidates must complete underwater and diving training as well as EMT courses.

medical terminology, cardiopulmonary resuscitation (CPR), weapons, PJ history, and leadership reaction. Trainees will attend Jump School, Combat Divers School, Underwater Egress Training, Survival School, and Free Fall Parachutist School.

They will additionally attend a twenty-two-week Paramedic Course at Kirtland AFB in Albuquerque, New Mexico, to learn how to treat and evacuate trauma patients. Graduates receive an EMT-Paramedic certification through the National Registry, the same as civilians.

The Pararescue Recovery Specialist Course requires an additional twenty-four weeks at Kirtland AFB. It includes training in how to treat patients in the field, field tactics, mountaineering, combat tactics, advanced parachuting, and helicopter insertion and extraction.

SO WHAT'S THE WEATHER LIKE?

Special Operations Weathermen are no ordinary meteorologists. They may need to fight their way near or inside enemy lines to carry out their weather report and must have the same training as all Air Force Weathermen.

Special Operations weather training includes AFSOC's Advanced Skills Training conducted at Hurlburt Field. No combat unit needs a surprise in weather conditions. Special Operations Weathermen are among the most highly trained members of the U.S. military. They must maintain the same weather weapon system qualifications as all Air Force Weathermen, in addition to the advanced special-tactics skills required of Special Operators. They attend more than a year of training overall and learn unique mission skills that earn them the right to wear the gray beret.

Special Operations Weathermen training begins with Jump School, a course in SERE tactics, and a course in water survival. What follows is a six-week course in how to operate inside both hostile and friendly territory. Trainees will learn communications, navigation, weapons, small-unit tactics, and other skills. Six months of advanced training follows at the Air Force Special Operations Command Advanced Skills Training course. There, trainees are taught to become warriors who can survive and operate in all climates and situations, day or night. Next, trainees attend a two-week Special Operations Weather Selection Course, where they learn about sports physiology, nutrition, and the history and basics of Special Operations weather.

Special Operations Weather Initial Skills Course is at Keesler AFB in Mississippi. It consists of twenty-nine weeks of training that includes basic, intermediate, and advanced meteorology, creating meteorological reports, and computer operations. Topics in meteorological training include weather chart analysis, weather radar, tropical meteorology, synoptic lab, weather equipment, and much more. Trainees will learn to comprehend investigative meteorology and weather prediction techniques. This is the same course that all

Special Operations Weathermen are the first ones in a jump zone. The information they supply ensures that conditions are right for other Special Ops Forces to get boots on the ground safely.

53

Air Force Weathermen trainees take, except that it includes progressively more difficult fitness training.

Special Operations Weather Apprentice Course at Fort Bragg's Pope Field is a thirteen-week course that provides final Special Operations weather qualifications. In addition to physical training and severe weather operations, trainees are prepared in small-unit tactics, land navigation, communications, demolitions, and field operations. Military meteorologists will face the same combat hazards as other forces and must be prepared.

Special Tactics Advanced Skills Training is a twelve-month program at Hurlburt Field in Florida. Newly assigned Special Operations Weathermen will become mission-ready Operators during this time by focusing on initial skills, core tasks, and operational-readiness training with rigorous mental and physical training.

SKILLS TAKE TIME TO LEARN

Tactical training for Special Ops demands greater mental and physical stamina, endurance, resilience, and discipline than you may ever have believed possible. You will be tested constantly and in the most arduous of circumstances. But if you survived the grueling training for any one of these Special Operations Forces, you will be one of a unique few ready when the leader says, "This is not a drill."

GLOSSARY

AIRBORNE Of or relating to troops trained to parachute or land in a combat zone or hostile territory.

BASE An area from which military operations are launched or supported.

BASIC TRAINING The minimum instruction and initial training new military recruits must endure. Physical training and courses in warfare are usually covered during this phase.

BATTALION An organized group of troops who act in coordination with each other.

CHALK A non-specific number of men who fit in a plane on any given day. They line up to the chalk line to jump.

COMBAT CONTROL TEAM A group of Special Operations Forces certified as air traffic controllers who are trained to deploy into hostile environments and establish and control assault zones and airfields.

COUNTERTERRORISM Direct and indirect actions taken against terrorism.

DEPLOYMENT The rotation of forces into and out of an area of conflict or combat.

FREE FALL A jump in which a parachute is activated either manually or automatically at a predetermined altitude.

GUERRILLA WARFARE Unconventional warfare usually carried out by small groups of forces who are often independent.

HYPOTHERMIA A medical condition in which the body's temperature falls far below normal.

INTELLIGENCE Information about foreign nations or hostile or potentially hostile forces that was gathered and examined by experts. Also referred to as "intel."

JUMPMASTER The designated airborne-qualified individual who directs paratroopers on an aircraft until they exit.

METEOROLOGY The study of the atmosphere and weather or weather-related phenomena, including applying physics, chemistry, and dynamics to understanding the effects of the atmosphere on the Earth's surface and the oceans.

OPERATION A sequence of planned actions with a common purpose or unifying theme. A military action or mission.

RAPPEL To descend on a slope or from a mountain by sliding down a rope and using one's feet to push against the surface of the slope.

RECONNAISSANCE A military mission to observe and gather information on the activities and resources of an enemy or adversary, or of a particular area. Also called "recon."

RUCKING Walking at a fast pace in boots and uniform over rough terrain carrying a weapon and a backpack weighing at least 45 pounds (20.4 kg).

SMALL ARMS Easily portable weapons used mainly against personnel and lightly armored or unarmored equipment.

FOR MORE INFORMATION

Department of National Defence and the Canadian
   Armed Forces
National Defence Headquarters
Major-General George R. Pearkes Building
101 Colonel By Drive
Ottawa, ON K1A 0K2
Canada
(888) 995-2534
Website: http://www.forces.gc.ca
The Department of National Defence and the Cana-
   dian Armed Forces advise and support Canada's
   Minister of National Defence and provides infor-
   mation on training and education opportunities in
   Canada's Armed Forces.

The Royal Military College of Canada
13 General Crerar Crescent
Kingston, ON K7K 7B4
Canada
(613) 541-6000, ext. 6302
Website: http://www.rmc.ca
The Royal Military College of Canada prepares students for service in Canada's Armed Forces and
   offers training in military tactics, fortification,
   and engineering and helps build scientific knowl-
   edge connected to military training.

United States Naval Academy
121 Blake Road
Annapolis, MD 21402
(410) 293-1520
Website: http://www.usna.edu/homepage.php
The U.S. Naval Academy prepares young men and
women to serve in the U.S. Navy and U.S. Marine
Corps. Its curriculum integrates physical and aca-
demic training.

United States Special Operations Command
(USSOCOM)
7701 Tampa Point Boulevard
MacDill Air Force Base, FL 33621
(813) 826-4600
Website: http://www.socom.mil/default.aspx
USSOCOM oversees the various Special Operations
Forces of the U.S. military. It also provides information on educational opportunities for members
of Special Ops as well as an advocacy program and
outreach for injured members and their families.

WEBSITES

Because of the changing nature of Internet links,
Rosen Publishing has developed an online list of websites related to the subject of this book. This site is
updated regularly. Please use this link to access the
list:

http://www.rosenlinks.com/ISF/Tact

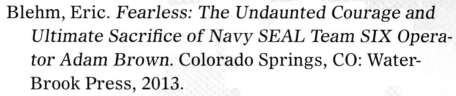

Blehm, Eric. *Fearless: The Undaunted Courage and Ultimate Sacrifice of Navy SEAL Team SIX Operator Adam Brown.* Colorado Springs, CO: WaterBrook Press, 2013.

Hawke, Mykel. *Hawke's Green Beret Survival Manual.* New York, NY: Running Press, 2012.

Luttrell, Marcus, and James D. Hornfischer. *Service: A Navy SEAL at War.* New York, NY: Back Bay Books, 2014.

Mooney, Michael J. *The Life and Legend of Chris Kyle: American Sniper, Navy SEAL.* New York, NY: Little, Brown and Company, 2013.

Owen, Mark, and Kevin Maurer. *No Easy Day: The Autobiography of a Navy SEAL.* New York, NY: Dutton Adult, 2012.

Pushies, Fred. *MARSOC: U.S. Marine Corps Special Operations Command.* Minneapolis, MN: Zenith Press, 2011.

Schwalm, Tony. *The Guerrilla Factory: The Making of Special Forces Officers, the Green Berets.* New York, NY: Simon & Schuster, 2013.

Shelton, Peter. *Climb to Conquer: The Untold Story of WWII's 10th Mountain Division Ski Troops.* New York, NY: Scribner, 2011.

United States Army Ranger Regiment. *Ranger Athlete Warrior 4.0: The Complete Guide to Army Ranger Fitness.* CreateSpace Independent Publishing Platform, 2013.

BIBLIOGRAPHY

Beckwith, Charlie A., and Donald Knox. *Delta Force: A Memoir by the Founder of the U.S. Military's Most Secretive Special-Operations Unit*. New York, NY: William Morrow, 2013.

Clark, Josh. "How the Green Berets Work" Retrieved March 1, 2014 (http://science.howstuffworks.com/green-beret.htm).

Couch, Dick. *Always Faithful, Always Forward: The Forging of a Special Operations Marine*. New York, NY: Berkley, 2014.

Lusted, Marcia Amidon. *Army Delta Force: Elite Operations* (Military Special Ops). Minneapolis, MN: Lerner Publishing, 2013.

Military.com. "Army Special Forces Training." Retrieved February 4, 2014 (http://www.military.com/special-operations/army-special-forces-training.html).

Military.com. "Joining the Army Special Forces." Retrieved February 4, 2014 (http://www.military.com/special-operations/joining-the-army-special-forces.html).

Payment, Simone. *Black Ops and Other Special Missions of the U. S. Navy SEALs* (Inside Special Forces). New York, NY: Rosen Publishing, 2013.

Poolos, J. *Black Ops and Other Special Missions of the U. S. Marine Corps Special Operations Command* (Inside Special Forces). New York, NY: Rosen Publishing, 2013.

Scarborough, Rowan. "Delta Force: Army's Quiet Professionals." *Washington Times*, June 3, 2012. Retrieved January 3, 2014 (http://www.washingtontimes.com/news/2012/jun/3/delta-force-armys-quiet-professionals/?page=all).

Shea, Therese. *Black Ops and Other Special Missions of the U.S. Army Green Berets* (Inside Special Forces). New York, NY: Rosen Publishing, 2013.

Sodaro, Craig, James C. Bradford, and Heidi A Burns. *The U.S. Marines Special Operations Regiment: The Missions* (American Special Ops). Oak Park, CA: Velocity Books, 2012.

United States Navy and Marine Corps. *Survival, Evasion, Resistance And Escape Student Handbook*. Survival Ebooks, 2011.

U.S. Air Force. "Inside AFSOC." Retrieved December 14, 2013 (http://www.afsoc.af.mil/specialtactics).

U.S. Army. "Soldier Life: Airborne School." Retrieved January 13, 2014 (http://www.goarmy.com/soldier-life/being-a-soldier/ongoing-training/specialized-schools/airborne-school.html).

U.S. Marine Corps. "MARSOC SERE Required Gear List." Retrieved February 5, 2014 (http://www.marsoc.marines.mil/Portals/31/Documents/MARSOC_SERE_Full_Spectrum_Required_Gear_List.pdf).

U.S. Navy. "Navy SEAL Training (Navy SEAL Boot Camp)—Weeks 1–3." September 4, 2009. Retrieved February 27, 2014 (http://information.usnavyseals.com/2009/09/navy-seal-training-navy-seal-bootcamp---weeks-1-3.html).

INDEX

ABOUT THE AUTHOR

Mary Blount Christian graduated from the University of Houston with a degree in journalism and worked as a reporter for *The Houston Post* before retiring to write more than one hundred fiction and non-fiction books for children and adults. She taught creative writing at Houston Community College, on the local PBS station KHTV in Houston, and at Rice University's School of Continuing Studies.

PHOTO CREDITS

Designer: Brian Garvey; Editor: Shalini Saxena